(Alas de Fe)

by
Mario J. Zani

Beacon Hill Press of Kansas City
Kansas City, Missouri

Copyright 2002
by Beacon Hill Press of Kansas City

Printed in the United States of America

ISBN 083-411-9412

Cover Design: Ted Ferguson
Illustrator: Gary Mowry

Editor: Donna Manning
Associate Editor: Kathleen M. Johnson

Note: This is a fictional account of actual people and events. It is part of the *Understanding Christian Mission,* Children's Mission Education curriculum. It is designed for use in Year 2, The Bible and Mission. Lessons focus on the Bible and how it helps missionaries tell others about God's love.

10   9   8   7   6   5   4   3   2   1

Contents

1

Preparing for a Big Event

"Dad! Dad!" yelled Luis [LEW-is] as he ran from the street to the patio. Felipe [fay-LEE-pay] put the hammer down and smiled at his son. He had almost finished the guest bathroom.

"Dad, they're bringing the new beds for our guests!"

"That's good," replied Felipe. "Tomorrow district leaders will arrive to attend district assembly. Our church must be ready."

Felipe was the pastor of the church and a respected leader in the community.

"Dad, will a lot of people come?" asked Luis.

"Yes, Son," answered Felipe as he climbed down the ladder. "This is a very special occasion. Now let's go help with the mattresses."

Pastors and members of the churches would soon be arriving in San Cristobal [sahn kris-TOH-bahl], Guatemala to celebrate this

special event. Some would hike through mountains and cross rivers to attend the assembly.

Children would come too. They were always excited to see their friends. Everyone looked forward to this time together. The people enjoyed the preaching and the singing. Some people would bring guitars and marimbas [mah-RIM-bahs].

The Guatemalan people love music! There is music everywhere—on the streets, in the city markets, and in the mountains. There would be music at the assembly too!

Felipe and Luis helped the men place the mattresses in the two Sunday School rooms. "This is where the general superintendent, the missionary, the translator, and the pilot will stay," said Felipe.

"Dad, do you remember what happened last year?" Luis asked as they walked back to the patio. "The special guests could not come because the road between our village and Coban [coh-BAHN] was closed," recalled Luis.

"That's right," said Felipe. "During the rainy season, there are places in Guatemala where it rains for days and even weeks. Many roads are closed because of landslides."

Felipe climbed the ladder to finish the roof.

"Son, this year will be different. Even if it rains, the special guests will come. We now have an airplane that can transport them."

"That's great, Dad! I hope the sky is clear when they fly."

"Well, the sky is not clear now," said Felipe. "There's a thunderstorm approaching, and it's starting to rain. We should go inside. I'll tell you a story about how the aviation ministry began in Guatemala."

"OK, Dad. I'll go get Monica and Rafael [RAH-fay-el]. They'll want to hear a story about the pilots and the planes too!"

Felipe put his hammer away. "Hurry, Luis. It is raining harder. Tell Mom we'll be in the church until the rain stops."

2

An Exciting Story

"Are you ready to hear the story?" Felipe asked.

"Oh, yes!" said Luis and his two friends, Monica and Rafael. They gathered around Felipe.

"The story begins with a missionary pilot named John Sprunger. He flew his plane all the way from the United States across the Atlantic Ocean to Africa."

"Wow! That's a long trip!" exclaimed Monica.

"It sure is," Felipe continued. "It is a very long trip. But John made a stop in Guatemala. He met with Dr. Mario Zani, the regional director, and other missionaries, including Mark Ryan. They discussed plans to start an aviation ministry in our country."

"Dad," Luis interrupted, "planes are expensive! "

"That's true, Son," Felipe replied. "The leaders had other expenses too. They had to plan for gasoline, parts, and maintenance for the plane. They needed a place to keep the plane. And, they wanted a place where the pilot and his family could live."

Rafael asked Felipe, "Where would Dr. Zani get the money to pay for everything?"

"Our church is known for its generosity," Felipe said. "When there is a need, Nazarenes, including children, are happy to use their time and money to help others."

"How did children help?" Monica asked.

"I'll answer that in a minute." Felipe continued, "Dr. Zani and Mark Ryan knew it was difficult to reach some churches by land. It could take up to 12 hours. And that's when the roads were in good condition! So, even though it would be expensive, Dr. Zani and Mark believed that air travel was the answer."

"Oh, I get it!" Luis exclaimed. "It would be easier to reach those churches by plane since there are many runways already built in this country."

"It's true," said Rafael. "There's a runway nearby!"

"Exactly," Felipe replied. "There are many runways in Guatemala where small planes can land."

"What kind of cargo would this plane carry?" Rafael asked.

Felipe smiled. Luis and Monica chuckled. "Very special cargo," Felipe explained. "This airplane could bring teachers to train our pastors, materials for Work and Witness teams, projection equipment for *JESUS* film teams, and . . ."

"Oh, I saw that film," Luis told Rafael.

"Me too," said Monica.

"Most of us have seen it," said Felipe. "But if the missionaries had a plane, they could take the *JESUS* film to other mountainous villages.

"However, at that time, there wasn't

enough money to purchase a plane. So, Dr. Zani, Mark Ryan, and John Sprunger prayed. All of them agreed that if God wanted an aviation ministry in Guatemala, He would supply the money."

3

Wings for the Gospel

The storm outside grew stronger. The thunder rumbled. And the raindrops on the roof became louder. Felipe raised his voice and continued his story.

"Dr. Zani decided to ask the church leaders in Kansas City for help. He wrote letters to Louie Bustle, the World Mission director, and Nina Gunter, the director for Nazarene Missions International.

"Many months passed. He didn't know if their idea to have an aviation ministry in Guatemala would be accepted or not," Felipe explained.

"So, even if they had money, they couldn't just go buy a plane?" Monica asked.

"That's right," Felipe responded. "First, someone had to study the advantages and disadvantages of the new ministry. Then, they had to write contracts and procedure manuals. Finally, someone had to approve the ministry."

"And they did, right, Dad?" Luis asked.

"The ministry was approved," Felipe answered. "Immediately after that, plans were made to raise the money for a plane. Children were encouraged to participate."

Luis, Monica, and Rafael looked at each other. "Children?"

"Children don't have money!" Rafael exclaimed.

"They had faith," Felipe said. "Do you know what faith is?" he asked.

"Yes," Monica answered. "My Sunday School teacher taught us that faith is trusting in God and totally depending upon Him and His promises. We have faith that God will work through us to help others."

"Very good answer!" exclaimed Felipe.

"How does God do that?" asked Rafael.

"Good question," said Felipe. "Children around the world participated in a project called, *Wings for the Gospel*. The church asked children to give offerings to buy the airplane."

"I'm sure they didn't get enough money to do that!" Rafael interrupted.

"Do you remember when you were asked to bring a rooster or a dozen eggs to our church?" Felipe asked.

"Yes," they replied in unison.

"My mom gave me a hen," Monica said. "But before I got to church, it escaped. I'm glad my uncle was nearby. He caught it for me!"

They all laughed.

"Well," Felipe continued, "you were helping to raise money for *Wings for the Gospel*. In a similar way, the Church of the Nazarene was able to raise money from around the world to buy a plane for Guatemala. And there was enough money left to buy a second plane for Africa."

"That's incredible, Dad! And Rafael didn't think they'd get enough money," Luis teased.

"When children trust in God, they can accomplish many important things for Him," Felipe said with a smile. "Because of you, as well as Nazarene children around the world, the plane will be landing here tomorrow!"

4

A Hangar and a Home

"It looks like the storm is almost over. I need to go back to work on the roof."

"Oh, please finish telling us the story," pleaded Monica. "Well, perhaps you should know that buying the plane wasn't as easy as it seemed. There were some problems."

"What kind of problems, Dad?"

"Before they bought the plane, they had to find a pilot. The Sprunger family became the missionaries in this region, and John agreed to become the pilot," answered Felipe.

"So the problem was solved, right?" Rafael asked.

"No, there was another problem," Felipe continued. "It cost too much to rent a hangar at the Aurora Airport in Guatemala, so the plane would have to sit outside without protection."

"Oh, I know why the pilot was worried," said Rafael. "People could damage the plane."

"That's right," Felipe told Rafael. "But God helped the leaders find the answer. One day, Mark Ryan saw a friend at the airport. He was selling his hangar at half price."

"That's great! They bought it, right?" Monica asked.

"No," Felipe replied. "It was still too expensive. They didn't have enough money."

"So, what did the leaders do?" asked Rafael.

"After talking some more, the owner decided to lower the price. The leaders were able to pay for the hangar. God worked through many people."

"Neat!" exclaimed Luis.

"I wouldn't call it neat," said Felipe. "The hangar had been abandoned. There was no running water, and it needed repairs on the inside and the outside.

"But God answered prayer. Electricians and construction workers from Sterling, Illinois, repaired the hangar. Today it is one of the nicest in Guatemala."

"What about the pilot?" Rafael asked.

"Ah, yes. One of the most important concerns was where the Sprunger family would

live. Again, God answered prayer. Work and Witness teams built a house for the Sprunger family near the airport." Felipe smiled. "This was another miracle from the Lord and a reminder that faith gives us hope."

"Dad, it's stopped raining!" Luis exclaimed.

Felipe stood up. "I'd better get back to work."

"But," Monica protested, "we want to know the rest of the story."

"All right," Felipe said. "Help me finish getting ready for the assembly tomorrow. Tonight, before dinner, I'll finish the story."

5

Help When Help Is Needed

"Delivery for the pastor!" shouted the messenger.

Felipe climbed down the ladder and walked out to meet him. "Good news?" Felipe asked.

"I think so," he replied. "This came over the radio a little while ago from Mark Ryan. It says: 'I will be in San Cristobal tomorrow. Dr. Jim Bond and his wife and John Hall, the translator, will be with me. Please meet us at the airstrip.'"

Felipe was thrilled with the news.

"Dad!" Luis called as Felipe climbed back up the ladder. "We've finished cleaning. Will you finish the story?"

"Very well. Go back to the sanctuary, and I'll be there in a few minutes. I have to put the tools away," Felipe told them.

A few moments later, the four of them sat in the church. Felipe continued his story.

"Many years ago, there was a young man from Guatemala who was a Nazarene. He went to school and studied English and aviation mechanics. He became one of the best Cessna mechanics in Central America.

"Mark Ryan met this young man, Alejandro Alvarez. Mark didn't know he was Cessna's chief mechanic. What a surprise for both of them when Alejandro introduced himself and Mark told him about the new ministry!"

"Then what happened?" Monica asked.

"Alejandro told Mark he had his own shop at the airport. He said he had prayed for many years that the Church of the Nazarene would begin an aviation ministry in Guatemala. Do you know what happened?" Felipe asked the children.

"No!" the three of them answered in unison.

"Alejandro offered to be a mechanic for the plane free of charge," Felipe replied. "He also said he would be able to get parts for the plane at half price. What do you think of that?"

"Dad, that's awesome!" exclaimed Luis.

"Yes, God is an awesome God. The plane

arrived only a few months ago. Already it has flown to Honduras, El Salvador, and many places in Guatemala. It has delivered medicine and food to families who were affected by Hurricane Mitch and the earthquake. And . . . ," Felipe added, "the plane was officially dedicated in a special ceremony in Guatemala City."

"What do you mean officially dedicated?" Luis asked.

"In a special ceremony, people prayed and asked God to bless the plane and those involved with its ministry. The plane's name was chosen from a list of names submitted by children," Felipe explained.

"What's the name of the plane?" Rafael asked, excitedly.

"*Alas de Fe.* It means Wings of Faith," Felipe replied. "Sarah Torrez, an eight-year-old girl from Houston, Texas, was among the hundreds who sent in a name. Hers was the one chosen. Sarah was invited to sit in the plane and have her picture taken."

* * *

"*Bbbrrrrrrrrrrrrrrrrrrr,*" the sound of the Cessna T-210 could be heard by people in the

village of San Cristobal. It was almost noon when the plane flew over the church.

"Let's go!" yelled Luis. He and his friends ran toward the truck where his dad waited. "The missionaries are here."

They climbed into the back of the truck, and Felipe drove them to the airstrip. The passengers and the pilot were already unloading their luggage from the plane.

Felipe parked next to the Cessna. The children jumped out and ran toward the plane. Felipe got out and walked toward the guests to introduce himself. Soon, more of the town's people began to arrive.

"Welcome!" Felipe called. "It is good to meet you and see the new plane, *Alas de Fe*! We were sure you would make it to district assembly this year!"